Magic
Of
Simply
Falling
In
LOVE

Poetry
and
Prose

-Swastik Chandel

To all the lovers,

who're waiting for love,
who taught different love,
who lived love,
this - for you all, for everyone.

How ironic, i don't have enough words (i'm a writer) to
express a big gratitude to my family, friends and of course to
all of you, you inspire me,
thank you,

Thank You So Much.

" Radhey Radhey "

Themes

Chapter 1

Sometimes you actually have to slip in love before you fall in love.

We slip away from worries and all,
into lurries of affection, gentle and tall.
The first stage, a romantic call,
slipping into love, the greatest of all.

Picture it as a poetic dive into the waves of love.
This first chapter is an exploration of the myriad emotions,
feelings and experiences that define the initial descents.
Within these pages, you'll discover a collection of heartfully
crafted (my effort) poetries and prose, each a lyrical ode to
the various facets of falling in, ofc ' *El - Oh - Wie - Ee* '.
Its like a soundtrack to those heart-flipping moments, that are
close to your 'aorta . From time freezing eye contacts to
stumbling through the first awkward conversations, laying it
all bare in verse.
Woven seamlessly, all the words, i hope will guide you
through the tender intricacies of spending time with a
newfound love, from the nervous excitement of that inaugural
date to the nuanced beauty of matured love.
And yeah! there's more,
sprinkled between this poetic humming there's a
conversation/a word on, on what it's reflecting, followed by
my real life experiences quoted as prose inbetween.

I share some of my feels, that i hope you'll love to visualize.
So, grab a comfy seat and join me in this casual stroll through
the ' crazy beautiful mess ' called as ' magic of simply falling
in love '.

Disclaimer

Age of 21, I find myself standing before you with a limited
span of life experiences, particularly in the realm of love.
But surely I can assure you that I have approached the subject
with an open heart, have explored love from every possible
perspective that my limited years could afford, embracing the
diverse narratives and lessons that have come my way.
I've put my heart into these pages, trying to capture all the
love vibes I've soaked up so far in my 21 trips around the sun.
But let me tell you, it was a rollercoaster putting it all down.
Going through the highs and lows, revisiting every laugh,
every tear - it was like diving headfirst into my own emotional
pool. Kinda mixed, but totally worth it.
I've poured into this book the love that has graced my life
until now, love, in all its forms, whether it be the warmth of
family, the camaraderie of friends, or the bittersweet
symphony of romantic entanglements.
And I genuinely hope you enjoy the perspective I bring to this
conversation.

' first glimpse of yours '

In the moment our eyes kissed,
clocks stood still,
A love story started,
against my will.

Your glare spoke volumes, a silent song,
in that moment, love came along.
Wasn't ready for the smile you'd show,
yet there you were, giving my feelings a flow.

Universe whispered in that quite stare,
a beat of hearts, beyond compare.
To unknown feeling,
i surrendered to the unknown,
Not knowing where,
our love would be sown.
All i knew,
that first glimpse of yours,
I was just yours,
I was all yours.

Words on
' first glimpse of yours '

Have you ever felt the world pause, the clocks stop ticking, something like that ?

Have you ever felt, time holding its breath specially when you lock eyes with someone for the very first time ?

Most of you would've been in such a place where this thing actually happens. And if someone have not, let me tell yaa, yaa it happens.

What happens actually is, the perception that time slows when locking eyes accidently with someone you love is often scientifically attributed as heightened emotional experience. Intense emotions, such as love, can trigger the release of some kind of hormones. These hormones affect our brain's perception of time, and we may feel time is stretching or slowing (for a short period of time).

But this is ofc scientific, whatever the reason could be, *what's important, is the way it happens.*

And believe me, It's like a magical suspension. In that fleeting moment, you're taken to a place you've never been before, a realm where your heart whispers, *"This is it".*

In that timeless moment, it's as if a new chapter begins.

An unimaginable, an 'unfamiliar yet comforting feeling'.

Something that you were supposed to find, and something that was supposed to find you.

Love becomes the extraordinary start we never knew we needed, an emotion unparalleled and unmatched. It's the unspoken understanding that, this is what we've been waiting for all long. Something nameless, yet already belonging.
In that fleeting gaze, we willingly surrender to the unknown. Despite the uncertainty, *we embrace the beauty of falling, without a safety.*
Love beckons us to a place beyond imagination, promising an incredible journey. We let it carry ourselves to *somewhere different, somewhere beautiful, somewhere we belong to, but never knew.*
It's for those moments that make us wish time could stand still, and love could last forever. In that moment of eye contact, in that split second, you become theirs, embracing the uncertainty with open arms.

Here's something from my first :
(next page)

I wasn't expecting much that day,

never seeking the extraordinary in people,

I was never looking for what i got that day,

I cannot be more grateful for what i got that day - YOU

You basked in the glow of popularity within the corridors of

college,

I was mere a symphony of existence to you.

You - epitome of desires,

friends of you calculated proposals,

i use to calculate distance between us.

Amidst the lecture's monotony,

you were focusing on java,

i was focusing on ' how to talk to you '.

You were busy doing your thing,

when i asked for a help with code,

You forwarded the solution on whatsapp,

i whispered, ' i got the number '.

A picturesque moment,

you adjusting your spectacles to catch my eye.

Moment i'll never forget -

your smile,

when you noticed me noticing you.

Our initial eye contact was mere a glaze,

became the prologue to our tacit narrative,

an unspoken dialogue.

It was our first conversation,

our first kiss,

that stretched to an eternity of shared enchantment.

' this talking phase '

Sarcastic echoes teased, 'Had anything been
amiss?"
for in your voice, in you,
my senses found a bliss.
Our first conversation, Oh! this talking phase,
each second passing with individual grace.

I savor every nuance when you speak,
lips in motion, a language unique,
gesture of hands and expressive eyes,
spellbinding with each blink that flies.
Every word, stitching a song,
i could listen all day long.
In the company of love, in the company of
you,
my heart's comfort, i belong to you.

As the day ends,
how i try to sustain,
with hope in my gaze,
to be with you again.

Words on
' this talking phase '

Okayy, picture this :
you're in that initial phase of talking with a person you locked your eyes. You know that they know, its happening, and you both know that you're giving it a little go! letting universe set up pace and plot.
So, you know how does it feels like when it happens all naturally ? When *universe play an intentional hand in colliding the two 'meant to be' souls* ?
here,
Every word exchanged is like a sneak peek into a romantic novel you never knew you were a part of. Their voice ? its not just a sound; its a secret language that can make you do anything, that's why you hear them say, " what not people do in love ", sarcastic and a reality truth. But you know why ? because their voice melts your heart like, " Okay universe, where was this magic before ?"
Its when simple conversation transforms into a dialogues of emotions. Its the exhilarating phase of getting to know someone, a journey where
words become threads weaving a tapestry of connection.
With every conversation, you come closer and closer, the more you share with each other, the more you start feeling light. Talking to them becomes an addiction, a comforting habit. Their voice becomes soothing balm, a remedy to forget the stresses of the day.

Their presence feels like a warm hug to you. Its like your heart thanks you, for this voice you never knew you needed, for their giggling sound when it makes you smile more, for their calm hushes that makes you drifting on clouds.
And you know what's the cute part, i'll say, is the moment you find yourself noticing them, you start noticing the little things when they are speaking to you, like how their lips move, the subtle dance of their hands as they express themselves or that cute quirk of their eyebrow when they're amused, and those eyes ? each blink indicates background sound of the story that only the two of you are writing.
       - details that turn the ordinary conversations into gallery of love and fascination.
And as you head home, you're not just leaving; you're pressing pause on a movie and eagerly waiting to hit play button, romanticizing a sweet anticipation of the next 'yours conversation.

Here's something from my first :
(next page)

Unfamiliar faces, crowd and noise,

it was college's science day.

You and me fumbling up the stairs, on a quest to locate room

101,

lot of unknown faces, they were auditioning.

I saw you searched me amid the sea of unknown,

while i navigated through my audition.

Finally we collided, you with a jacket in your hand,

conversation ignited as if we were old friends catching up on

lost time.

Your words entered my ears but swirled in my stomach,

blooming butterflies,

lost in your presence,

heard nothin, blaming the background noise.

Seeking the solace from bustling chaos,

we sidestepped to a quite bench.

With a swift motion, you pulled out your phone, capturing a

moment that froze our newfound connection.

I gazed at your face through the phone's screen,

and in that selfie,

our first selfie,

my smile and your blush got a reason.

Your red blood sweater framed cheeks flushed with cherry

hue, as we exited the event with our elbows intertwined,

the world seemed to fade in the background,

while i tried to match your footsteps.

coffee

' colliding in circumstance '

Our first date, ofc i asked,
to something beautiful, we embarked.

Dawn looked back,
i was going to say,
sunset hues, a love display.
And your blush'ed- yes, echoed in the air,
feels burst, beyond compare.

The day witnessed, something pure,
sharing stories, laughter and more.
In every smile, a story untold,
eyes to explore, a hand to hold.
Thousands of conversations, a gentle dance,
two souls colliding in circumstance.

Heading home, a smile took place,
carrying a piece of you, a sweet embrace,
Heading home, with a heart so light,
you and me, felt so right.

Words on
' colliding in circumstance '

" I've really enjoyed our conversation, i was wondering if you'd be interested in grabbing coffee sometime. What do you think ? " Or

" I've been enjoying our time together, and i'd love to get to know you better. How about friday ? you and me ? "

Let's talk about those first times, first time you ask them for hanging out or for a date. It's *about the magical experience of first times*. The first time you go out with someone special, with someone you always wanted to.

Believe me! it's a feeling that wraps around you, like the warmth of sun on an accidental winter dayout. It feels like the world is just about the two of you. Everything falls into place, *everything around seems to conspire to make that moment uniquely yours*. Each moment with its own significance, making it all so worthwhile, that something in you whispers, ' *This is so worth it* '.

And you know what the best part is ?

when you gather all the courage to express your feelings, when you finally spill the beans about how you feel, with a heart dancing like hell with all the fingers crossed ,or, with all the veins crossed, cause that's how it feels in chest. Ofc there're chances & possibilities of either answer, but when all the things around you feels so right and feels so happening, then why not ask, cause inside you know the bottom line is you're in L O V E.

Cause believe me, *either answer will give you something, that'll be beautiful in it's own way.*

And when the answer is, yes, a ' YES ', it feels like everything stopped for a second, followed by world's favorite song playing in the background starting with a sweet violin, like everything around is celebrating with you. Then starts the never ending phase of countless conversations and shared laughter. And as you share time and stories, you realize you've found someone special, someone you'll look for in a crowd, someone who'll always be there, *a hand to hold, a heart to reside.*

And oh!, after that first time, that first magical day, on your way back home, you can't help but smile like you've got a secret, you smile like never before. There's *something about them, something beautiful, something serene,* that sticks with you.

Here's something from my first :
(next page)

In the echoes of the laughter, you and me and all our friends,

i noticed special moment, amidst the gentle rustle of your

hair,

with your lips holding hairpin,

and seized the courage to extend an invitation for a

rendezvous.

Your subtle nod, graceful dance of affirmation,

as i inquired, " on Friday ?"

set the scene for a lovely date.

The day of date, we spent the day chatting, subjects and

stories,

with an aromatic companionship of coffee.

As daylight waned, in the hushed tranquility,

even the dawn stopped by the scene,

as i rested my knee hurting on a pebble,

cause lost in your eyes,

and in thought of asking you,

with a flower with exact three petals.

The silence heard both of our heart beats fasting,

followed by the color of your cheeks.

A blush adorned your countenance with an ethereal grace,

and a short smile helped your lips to say that word,

that made me forget my knee was hurting.

' Yes ', carried the lightest weight of

hundreds of promises,

thousands of hugs and millions of kisses.

I returned home with a smile,

a reflection of yours,

and my lungs filled with your scent.

' first summer of us '

"Yes " echoed softly, in the first summer of us,
romance painted our hands with bluepink
brush.
Hands intertwined, inscribing memories,
sweat and hot streets, introducing territories.

Youtube recipes and pj mismatches,
resting between pillow fight matches.
Sharing memes, scenes and fav song,
Laying on each other, evenings long.
Movie nights, a cozy affair,
romancing each other with love to spare.

Summer waned, but the warmth endured,
as winter whispered, love matured.

Words on
' first summer of us '

So,

What after a ' yes ' ?

How does it feels like having someone, you can officially call your boyfriend/girlfriend ?

How does it feels like the blupink - begining of your relationship with your 'the one' ?

Let me tell you how the first summer goooes like, after 'finally' -

Summer's not just about the heat, its then, about the sizzle between young passionate souls.

Both of you holding hands, and the other side's the city. You with that sweaty arms roaming in the street, introducing to places together. Cafes and nature becomes the best hangout spots. But now it's not only about the city around, it's about hitting pause on time; you explore hidden spots just so you can have sweaty afternoon initials. Roadmap turns into your 'our canvas', *like with each step you're painting love* in the hues of setting sun.

Everything feels so going, so happening, like if something was missing, it was tasting different ice cream flavors with them while 33 degrees celsius.

And the afternoon endings ?

turns into a master chef finales as you go on experimenting different homemade dishes guided by youtube recipes. These brunches, works best while resting between pillow fights.

Followed by long summer evenings, that you spend discussing about your fav spotify artists, and sharing memes while laying on each other, marking bed territories.
And the nights when you binge your favorite movies and tv shows and discuss about alternate scenes, creating a cozy bubble *where it's just you two and time doesn't matter.*
As time passes by, there are career twists, problems, tough times, but you both always try to find the way out and support each other, to become the best version of yourselves. You understand the maturity of being in a relationship is *not only about having someone who's with you when you're laughing; it's also about having someone who stays when you're breaking in pieces.* It's about being there for each other, standing for each other and helping each other for facing fears and problems together, and finding the best solutions together. That's love.

Here's something from my first :
(next page)

In the quite corner of my room,

the soft strumming of my guitar painted the air with

anticipation,

glancing at the wall clock,

i eagerly awaited for your arrival.

Doorbell finally chimed, calling me it was you,

as you entered,

pressed my cheeks,

we shared a sweet kiss.

Evening unfolded with cocoa & choco cookies,

and kitchen witnessed a lot of kisses,

with a lot of mess.

Night draped its gentle veil,

we merged our blankets,

creating a cocoon.

The projector flickered by the magic of

Disney on the wall.

Movie marathon was half way,

feeling a pull of sleep,

you nestled into my lap.

I muted everything to hear your breathing.

Switching on the speakers,

slow song, slow volume,

while you whispered, 'perfect',

in your slumber.

I couldn't help but kiss your forehead,

as you purred while dreaming.

Surrendered to sleep, all i remember.

Morning unveiled your face,

your morning face,

radiant in its waking grace,

one of the most beautiful sights

i've ever known.

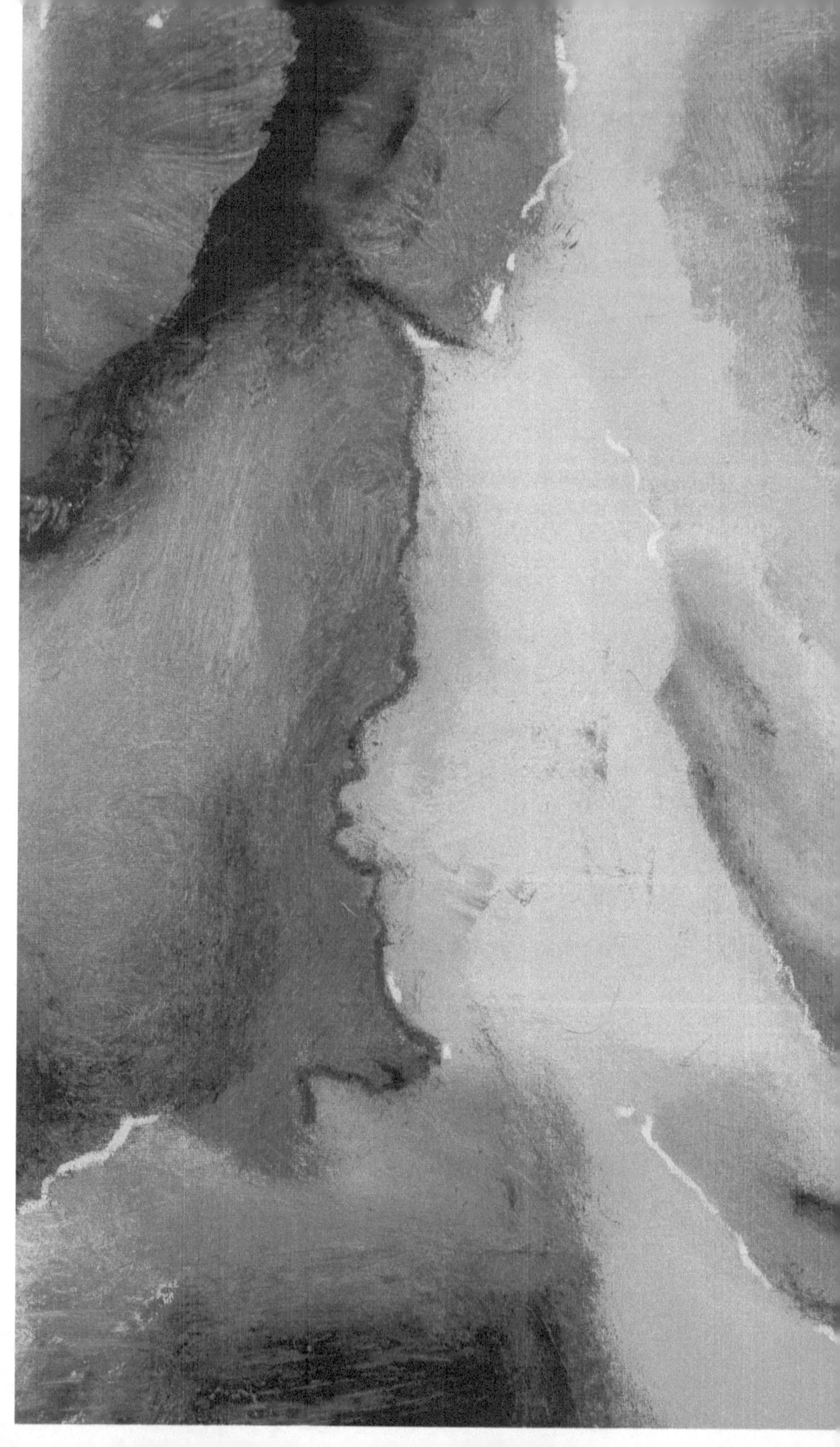

' blending love '

Blending, like hues in a canvas divine,
comfort settled, like aged, aged wine.

No fireworks blaze, nor thunderstorm roar,
yet, a symphony plays, a melody to adore.
In the comfort, a dance of souls combined,
love quietly blending, intricately entwined.

A flower vase delicate, handle with care,
for within its fragility, a love rare.
Hold onto the blend, like petals in a breeze,
for love matures, flourishing with ease.

Words on
' blending love '

Now let me walk you through the climax of the first chapter
with a discussion about this love thing (permanent one).
Love, that weathered the tests of time, emerging stronger,
more profound, that truly blended into *something
extraordinary, something about just two of you.*
You know, when its been a long way together, and you've
seen each other at your best and worst, but you're still
standing strong. When your relationship's a saga of
commitment, resilience and growth. Its a love that
acknowledges imperfections and embraces the beauty in even
ordinary details.This matured relation is formed with a
conscious choice to stay, to prioritize, to understand. Its
formed not only with strawberries alone, but with arguments
too, but also navigating them with grace and respect. This
love is not new anymore, yet it continually discovers novelty
in each other. Its not about the initial thrill anymore, but the
profound joy of uncovering new layers of affection and
admiration.
Its a love that evolves, not into monotony, but into a source
of perpetual excitement because, in every moment, you find
something new to love. Also, you both choose to set aside
room for growth, understanding that your individual
journeys are intertwined, making the collective journey richer
and more fulfilling. And as you celebrate special moments,
organize dates and bed for each other and create cherished
memories, its a testament to the intentional effort invested in
keeping the flame alive.

Its not about the grand gestures anymore (or can be), but more about the countless small acts of love that build the foundation of lasting bond.

Its the unique stage of your journey, where everything is about the comfort of permanence. Its like you've reached the supreme time, where love is not just a fleeting emotion; its a constant, a reliable force that shapes your days. Its like you've got your own rhythm, your own routine, and you wouldn't have it any other way.

As you grow and emerge as the dream couple you aspired to be, remember that this blending of love is an art - an ongoing masterpiece sculpted by shared experiences, understanding, and the unwavering commitment to building a life together. This one for shared dreams, shared responsibilities and above all, shared love.

And yes, there's no
" here's something from my first ", for this poetry, cause i feel i have not reached this point, i've yet to experience this kindof love. And i believe many of you can relate, so,
here's a beautiful short message instead;
for you all & to my self too :
(next page)

As you read this, i hope you're embracing the person you've become. The thing is, if you haven't found that epic love of yours, if you haven't encountered that mature & lasting love yet, don't rush it.
No need to go on a wild chase, just let the life do its thing. Focus on being awesome, loving yourself, enjoying the journey & ofc trust the timing of the universe. Your perfect love story will roll in when you'll be ready enough for this beautiful & magical connection.
So keep your heart open to every experience, and believe,
" Time is planning, it will take some time. "

And here's an advice,
Don't fall in love with your expectations, fall in love with the person, fall in love with them.
Open your heart to unexpected, allowing love to unfold organically. Embrace the beauty of accepting people as they are, without burdening them with your expectations. Talk to them and slowly fall in love with what they are, cause love is a unique journey, it's not about finding someone perfect but creating something beautiful together.
Start by ditching the checklist and let people surprise you.
And i'll say again, keep your heart open to new and random experiences, cause you never know, how and when you'll cross your paths with your ' the one '.
Love,
Love

Chapter 2 :
' Odyssey of love '

Seems like, our conversation,
we've come soo far on this path leading to love.
But the thing is, " we can only go as far as possible, cause i
guess love's not a station or destination, it's a journey ", a
never ending lovely journey.
Love's allure lies in its elusive nature; it cannot be fully
captured, described or lived in a standardized way, everyone
has experienced their own kindaa love, ofc different from one
another yet unique and beautiful in its own way, no rankings,
no comparison.
There's no hierarchy in the pursuit of love, some may stumble
upon this everlasting connection from the very beginning,
while others may discover it after enduring heartbreaks.
Every love story is complete and whole.

So, let me welcome you to this chapter, a journey through
verses and prose. No complex explanations, just lines woven
with heartfelt sentiments, lines about love, heartbreaks,
romance and everything in between, based on my experiences
and what i gained from other's experience.

Interpret every word of my poetry through your own lens,
regardless of the reasons or emotions i was experiencing.
Feel every word by your own perspective & let your own
thoughts fly between these pages.

23rd April

Shall i be your hairpin, cradling your scent in

each breath ?

Or a morning mug, or your lipstick,

touching your dry lips, sipped kisses ?

Or your brown sweater,

wrapping you in warmth ?

If within your atrium, my love,

i find my home where i belong,

would you let me stay ?

Or am i just a fleeting thought in your story, a

passing cloud ?

or a temporary refuge ?

Do you secretly wish for something,

or do you harbor expectations beyond my

capacity,

knowing you'll walk away in the end ?

Am i just a thread of sympathy

because i opened up ?

Tell me if i am anything more than an

echo ?

क्या ही पूछु ?
क्या मैं कुछ भी हूं तेरे लिए ?
उससे, जो मेरे लिए सब कुछ है।

03rd May

If my heart's a dry barren,

i'll grow 'you' flower from your heels

pierced on mine.

Still be afraid to touch,

for if, either i'll burst into delicate petals

or, cause you to wither.

If your phone,

not your alarm.

If your notes,

not syllabus.

If your sheet,

not the bed.

I Would

If i found

existence in you,

not existing for you,

I Would

To be you,

not to be me,

for, if my touch will cause a hairline crack;

i'll exist in you, not to be me.

तुम्हारे लिए होने से बढ़कर ,
तुम में होना है |

You should've stayed a bit,

i poured my heart into writing :

hundred love notes, places plans, and gifts

Just to show you, take you there star.

You should've stayed a bit,

I ain't the best at always displaying,

but sweet acceptance of love, proposal,

was to happen.

You should've stayed a bit,

i poured my heart into writing :

hundred love notes, places plans, and gifts,

buying you a butterfly necklace was

'one of them.

You should've stayed a bit

longer.

कुछ पल और ठहरते,

बहुत सी ख्वाइशें सजाई थी,

तुम्हें झुमके पहनाना उन में से एक था।

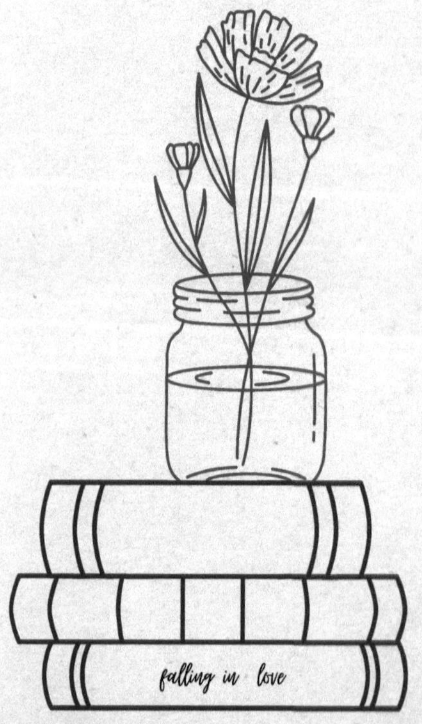
falling in love

How i wish to jump in,

to pluck that flower rare,

to fall in all in you, love;

But,

Instead, I'm just letting this affection grow,

much like the way that flower keeps getting

more beautiful every day, if i don't.

How i wish not to

mess with something beautiful, but still

wanting to be a part of it.

How i wish to

fall in love with the

essence, the growth, the grace;

instead of disturbing the

natural growth of affection.

How i wish to

fall in all in you, love.

बहुत कोशिश की तुम्हें हासिल करने की,

अब कोशिश रहेगी,

हिस्सा बनने की |

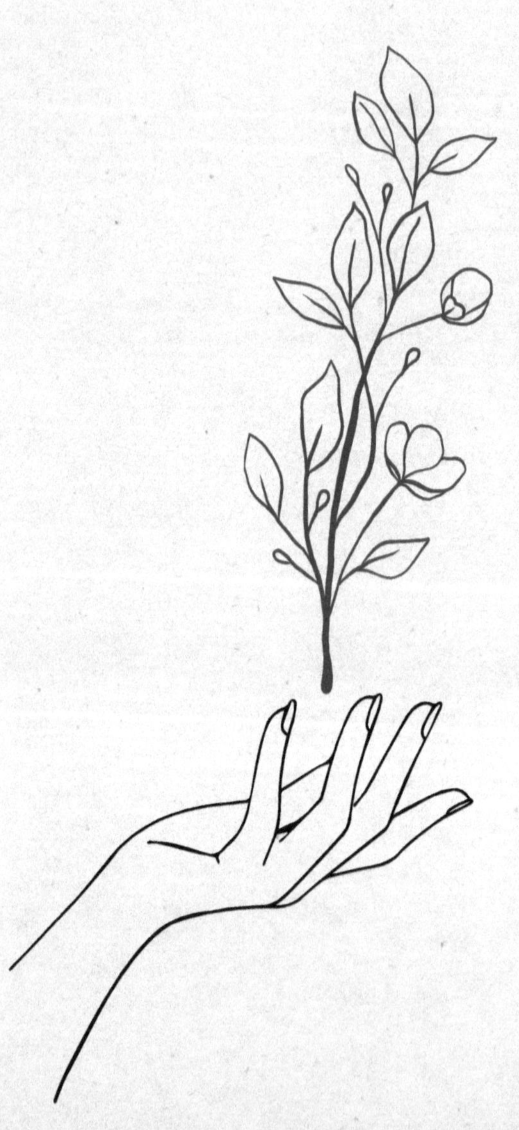

Realizing you're only mine

-my pride,

Declaring i'm only yours

-my love.

Not merely acquiring you,

-i love you,

But being completely yours,

-i love you.

Not in grand gestures,

only love, simple and true,

-in all that I do

Not about owning, it's about being,

In your love,

-in all that I do

-Love that lingers

until this very moment.

वो सिर्फ मेरा है, ये कहना भी सही।
मैं सिर्फ उसका हूं, ये कहना मोहब्बत है,

उसको सिर्फ पाना ही नहीं,
उसका होकर रहना भी मोहोब्बत है।
-ना जाने ये मोहब्बत कब तक है,
पर हाँ अब तक है।

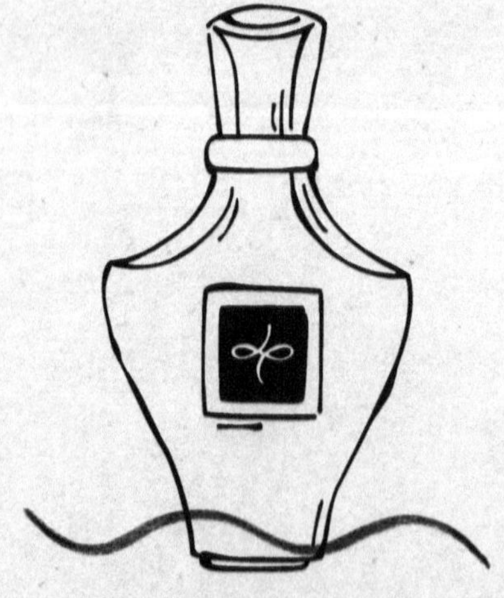

12th Dec

Haven't spoken to you in months,

we've been strangers more than we were

known, more than we were friends,

hard to say, yes i don't feel anything, but more

hard to let go of the

dreams we had together,

plans we had together &

times had together.

Haven't spoken to you in months,

haven't seen you in months,

hard to say i don't feel anything, but got to tell

you that

i still have your perfume,

your hairclip, your polaroid picture.

Haven't seen you in months,

hard to say i don't feel you & maybe i don't

even want you, but had to say,

it's always been you.

काफ़ी वक़्त लगा तुम्हें,

मुझे दिल से निकालने में;

फिर कहते हो प्यार नहीं था।

Flowers are still there,

but not my garden anymore;

I still walk through, sometimes,

sometimes I stay,

but not able to sense the scent

anymore.

Flowers are still there,

seems like, they don't recognize

touch,

they don't sense me anymore.

Flowers are still there,

not my anymore.

ना जाने क्यों भूलने लगा हूँ,

तुम्हें रोज़ देखना और तुम्हारा ना पहचानना,

तुम्हारी यादो को नहीं,

मैं तुम्हें भूलने लगा हूँ।

I was wondering under the starlit night,

if they were whispering about you ?

In the quiet, dark space, but when I tried to

listen,

it was not you, but anything.

I was wondering if your laughter lingered,

In the garden of dreams ?

where we use to run on the endless landscape,

but when i reached,

it was not you, but anything.

I was wondering if they still talk about us ?

fumbling through the pages of time,

as I flipped the page,

it was not you, but anything.

तुम वही हो,
मैं वही हूं,
पर अब हम नहीं हैं।

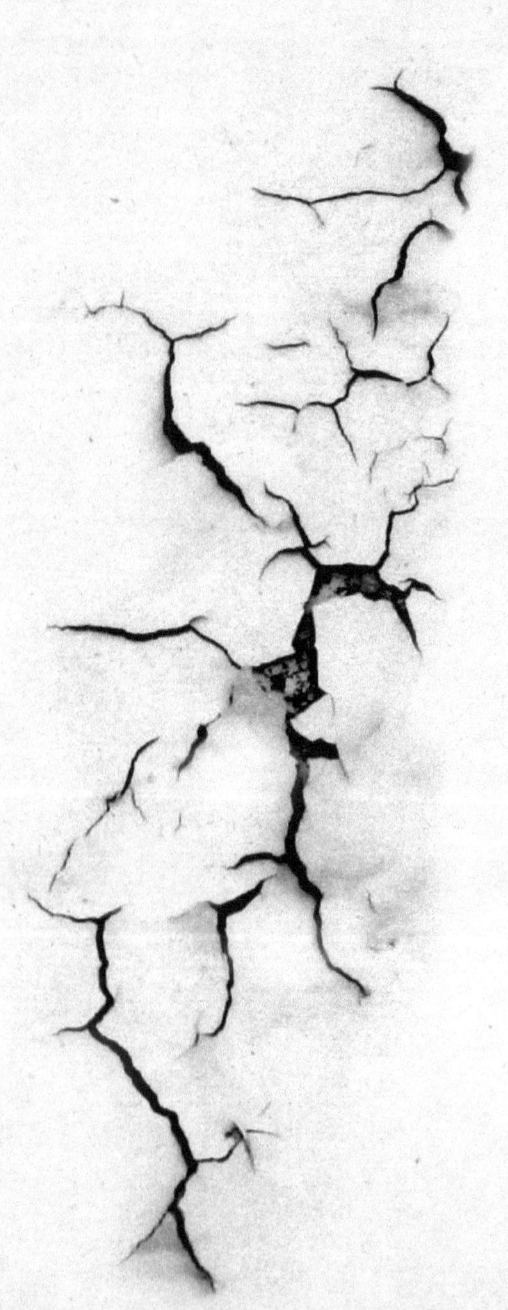

I looked in the mirror,

there was something in my eyes,

liquid sympathy form eyelids to cheeks,

I looked in, again,

there was broken image, trapped beneath,

not the mirror but me.

I looked back,

someone was helping me up,

getting me up,

who else, again,

I looked back,

it was me,

someone who wanted me to be better,

who else,

it was me.

दोबारा इसलिए नहीं,
कि मुझे डर भी है,
मुझे कीमत पता है, मैंने खुद को संभाला है।

I enquired, can you grow ?

from what you were,

from where you were,

you left your heart with ?

Answers were blur.

I self-doubted-ly asked, can i grow ?

from the comfort in darkness,

from draping my tears with rain,

from infinite scrolling ?

Answers were probable.

When I said I can,

watching my self worst,

i did.

टूटना बस मे नहीं था,
जुड़कर सुलझना है;
किस के लिए भला, किसी से शिकायत नहीं,
खुद जुड़ना है, खुद के लिए जुड़ना है।

My morning thought,

my eyes call,

my phone call,

my heart's comfort,

You were.

My favorites ? your every favorite,

my shirt, your perfume,

my routine,

my improvement,

You were.

you were.

तुम थे, अब नहीं हो,
शायद अब तुम, तुम भी नहीं हो।

I was sitting alone, no moon sky,

staring in the dark quite;

a shooting star from nowhere, lightened my

pupil.

I was laying and scrolling, vacuum room,

blue light and dark circles;

distant noise of my family chattering, the

second i was downstairs.

I was resting on my backpack, azure sky,

grass patches and insects sound:

Wind handling my hairstyle was my reason to

be quiet,

while an infant flower dancing was my reason

to smile.

आख़िरकार खुश रहना, हमारे हाथ ही तो है।

You're not there yet ?

It's Okay.

It's okay, you're way ahead.

-self

कोशिश और ज़िद

love

It's in the lyrics of the song,

that i dedicate to you;

In your smile,

when you notice me noticing you;

In the efforts towards each other,

when we do our best;

In the ego of our friends,

who knows us best;

In the conversation of stars,

there above,

lies the magic of simply falling in love.

एहसास >>>

Conversation with readers

Wow, what a ride, right ? I mean, who knew we could get so sentimental about strawberries and arguments, but here we are, feeling all the feels (i hope).

So, here we are at the end, and I gotta say, love is one heck of a trip. It's like this never-ending adventure, a journey with all its ups and downs, it isn't some checkmark on a checklist; it's more like a constant evolution, a story that keeps on writing itself. It isn't a one-size-fits-all kinda thing. It's messy, imperfect, and downright crazy at times, but that's what makes it beautiful, right? No rankings, no comparisons, just your own unique love story that's complete and whole in its own way. It's a saga that acknowledges imperfections, finds beauty in the ordinary, and thrives on the intentional effort invested in keeping the flame alive. And importantly It's about standing strong when life throws its curveballs. It's about choosing each other every single day, through thick and thin. Love, in all its forms, is resilient and enduring, a force that transcends the limitations of time and space.

Now as we delve into the final page of this poetic journey, remember, love is not confined to the pages of a book; it is a living, breathing entity that continues to unfold in our lives. So, let us embrace the lessons – to be awesome, to love ourselves, and to trust the timing of the universe when it comes to finding our own epic love story. It's a gentle encouragement to focus on yourself too, enjoy the journey, and believe that the perfect love story will unfold when we are ready.

As my words come to an end, let us carry the spirit of love
with us, cherishing the beauty of every experience and
remaining open to the magic that unfolds in its own time,
and may the magic of love perpetually grace our lives.
So, as we close the book (literally and metaphorically),
Thank you for your time, for embracing the sentiments
shared within these pages, and for being a part of this poetic
exploration of love. And yes! love won't end with my words –
it will persist, and so should we, in doing things that keep this
kind of love alive.
So stay healthy, stay happy, and may your days be filled with
the warmth and brilliance that love brings.

With Love and heartfelt wishes
for a future brimming with love,
Swastik

If you would like
to follow me on
Instagram - @bluewordsguy

a letter to yourself :